The Divine Psychological Journey

(©) Copyright 2023 by Ionuț-Alexandru Drăcea
All rights reserved.

The Divine Psychological Journey
Embracing Vulnerability

Ionuț-Alexandru Drăcea

"The journey of self-discovery often begins with a single question. In asking 'why?' we unlock the door to the deepest chambers of our minds, where vulnerability is embraced, and the divine complexities of our humanity are revealed."

(©) Copyright 2023 by Ionuț-Alexandru Drăcea

All rights reserved.

Published by

ISBN: 9798866509720

This book or any portion thereof may not be reproduced or used in any manner whatsoever without the express written permission of the publisher, except for the use of brief quotations in a book review.

Disclaimer:

This book serves a general informational purpose. Every endeavour has been undertaken to ensure the precision of the information presented; however, neither the author nor the publisher make any expressed or implied representations or warranties regarding the completeness, accuracy, reliability, suitability, or availability of the content. Any reliance on such information is at your sole risk.

This book does not aim to offer specific medical, legal, financial, or professional counsel. It is advisable for readers to seek professional advice or services when the need arises. The author and publisher cannot be held responsible for any direct, indirect, or consequential damages resulting from the use of this book or its content.

The opinions and perspectives expressed in this book belong to the author and may not necessarily reflect the official stance of any mentioned organization, entity, or individual. References to organizations, their policies, or their actions are founded on publicly available information and should not be misconstrued as endorsements or factual statements.

Under no circumstances will the author or publisher be liable for any claims, demands, or damages of any nature, including but not limited to those stemming from alleged breaches of intellectual property rights, defamation, or other legal claims related to the book's content.

For information, please contact:

www.draceasjourney.com/

Table of Contents

About the Author

Introduction: The Purpose of this Book

Chapter 1: SIGNIFICANCE OF EMOTIONAL RADAR

Chapter 2: IMPORTANCE OF ONLINE INTELLIGENCE

Chapter 3: THE MAIN CHARACTER SYNDROME

Chapter 4: THE SOCIAL MEDIA EXPERIMENT: EXPLORING THE IMPACT ON WELL-BEING

Chapter 5: NAVIGATING THE LABYRINTH: MODERN DATING

Chapter 6: THE DATING AND ITS EVOLUTIONARY PSYCHOLOGY

Table of Contents

Chapter 7: MATERIALISM, PERCEPTION, AND SOCIAL ANXIETY

Chapter 8: MAY I TAKE YOUR ORDER, PLEASE?

Chapter 9: DECISIONS IN THE HEART OF CARE: BALANCING LOGIC AND EMOTION

Chapter 10: LIGHTS, CAMERA, PSYCHOLOGICAL MANIPULATION

Chapter 11: INTUITION - SUFFOCATING OR DIVINE FEELINGS?

Chapter 12: A GRAND EXPERIMENT IN PERCEPTION

To You, Dear Reader

Meet the Author: *Ionuț-Alexandru Drăcea*

As we embark on this literary journey together, allow me to introduce myself. I am Alex, a dedicated nurse hailing from Romania, with a heartfelt mission to make a positive impact on the lives of individuals and families. My professional journey began in Romania, where I honed my skills as a nurse before embarking on an inspiring adventure to the UK.

My passion for helping others led me to specialize in dementia care, where I've had the privilege of providing compassionate support and guidance to those affected by this challenging condition. Within the realm of dementia care, I've become a mental wellbeing senator, committed to advocating for mental health awareness and support.

My role as a mental wellbeing senator is not just a title; it's a calling. I am dedicated to creating safe spaces for open conversations, where individuals can freely express their concerns, fears, and aspirations. Through workshops, impactful talks, and one-on-one consultations, I strive to empower individuals with the knowledge and tools necessary to navigate the complexities of mental wellbeing.

My journey is one of education, empowerment, and inclusivity. I believe in the transformative power of effective communication, active listening, and cultural sensitivity. These skills enable me to connect with diverse communities, fostering understanding and inclusivity in every interaction.

Within these pages, you'll find narratives that paint a portrait of me as a seeker of truth, a lover of knowledge, and a curator of stories that explore the quirks and complexities of our existence. I am a philosopher in the masquerade of life, inviting you to ponder the questions that have intrigued us since time immemorial.

Reader, you are not just embarking on a reading experience; you are stepping into a realm where curiosity knows no bounds, guided by the author of these extraordinary tales and reflections. Together, we shall unravel the threads of perception, embark on a psychological journey through the tales of Disney princesses, explore the subtle nuances of intuition, and contemplate the art of living authentically.

Welcome to this adventure.

A. Purpose of the book

Dear Reader,

Welcome to the pages of this book, a journey of exploration and understanding into the intricate realm of the human mind and the experiences that shape our psychological well-being. As you hold this book in your hands, know that you are not alone in your quest for self-discovery and emotional resilience. Together, we will embark on a path of empathy and knowledge, delving into the depths of our thoughts, feelings, and behaviours.

I chose to write this book because I believe in the power of connection and the importance of understanding ourselves and others on a deeper level. Throughout my own personal experiences and observations, I have come to realize that our psychological well-being is a fundamental aspect of our lives. Yet, it is often overlooked or misunderstood.

In a world that is increasingly fast paced, digitally connected, and filled with distractions, it is easy to lose sight of our own mental health.

We may find ourselves seeking validation in the virtual realm, comparing our lives to carefully curated social media feeds, and feeling the weight of societal pressures.

We may question our own worth, struggle with relationships, and grapple with the complexities of our emotions.

But fear not, dear reader, for this book is an invitation to delve into the depths of our psyche, to embrace our vulnerabilities, and to discover the incredible resilience that resides within us. It is an opportunity to unravel the mysteries of our thoughts and behaviours, and to navigate the challenges of our modern world with compassion and self-awareness.

Through the pages of this book, we will explore a wide range of psychological topics, from the intricacies of modern dating to the impact of social media on our well-being, and from the depths of depression to the heights of personal growth.

Each chapter will offer insights, reflections, and psychological explanations to help us better understand ourselves and the world around us.

In addition, we will delve into the fascinating topics of energy exchange and divine feelings. We will explore how our connections with others can shape our inner world and how those inexplicable sensations, sometimes bordering on the divine, can influence our thoughts and emotions.

But our exploration does not end here. In the following chapter, we will dive into the complexities of social media and the paradox of seeking online affection while facing the spectre of loneliness. We'll examine the psychological reasons behind this quest for affirmation and how it can impact our real-life interactions.

Moreover, we will diagnose what I like to call "The Main Character Syndrome," a phenomenon where online attention can lead to a distorted self-perception, isolating us from authentic human connections. We'll explore the insecurities that drive this syndrome and why we sometimes hide behind a character of our own creation.

Throughout this book, the purpose remains clear: to guide you on a journey of self-discovery, to encourage the embrace of your unique experiences, and to cultivate a deeper sense of empathy and understanding. Together, we will navigate the complexities of the human mind, seeking wisdom, connection, and the transformative power of self-reflection.

I am humbled and honoured to have you as a companion on this journey. As we embark on this exploration of the mind and heart, let us hold space for vulnerability, empathy, and growth. May this book serve as a guide, illuminating the path towards greater self-awareness, emotional well-being, and a deeper connection to the energies that shape our lives.

Dear reader, as you step into this realm, I implore you not to rush to judgment. The story unfolds on its own terms, unconstrained by traditional rules, making this book an experience unlike any other you've encountered. Let go of preconceived notions about books—lines, rules, and norms—because here, everything is different. Why, you might ask? The answers will become clear as you read along, with all secrets unveiled in our final chapter. Enjoy!

Drum roll, please!

Chapter 1-
SIGNIFICANCE OF EMOTIONAL RADAR

Emotional awareness, a concept that might seem deceptively simple at first glance, holds within its grasp the key to unlocking the intricacies of human interaction, personal growth, and mental well-being. In a world often driven by the hustle and bustle of daily life, pausing to delve into the realm of emotions might feel like a luxury. However, as we explore the depth and significance of emotional awareness, it becomes evident that this skill is not just a luxury – it's a necessity.

At its core, emotional awareness can be succinctly defined as the capacity to recognize, understand, and accept both your own emotions and those of others. It's the ability to tune into the emotional undercurrents that shape our thoughts, behaviours, and relationships. This awareness doesn't merely scratch the surface of our feelings; it delves deeper, uncovering the layers beneath each emotional response.

With emotional awareness, we become attuned to the nuances of emotions – from fleeting moments of joy to undercurrents of sadness, sparks of anger, and tides of calm.

It allows us to appreciate the complexities of the human experience and the rich tapestry of emotions that colour our interactions and decisions.

Emotional awareness stands tall as one of the cornerstones of emotional intelligence. It paves the way for other essential aspects of emotional intelligence to flourish, such as emotional regulation, empathy, and effective interpersonal relationships.

Imagine navigating a complex social landscape without the compass of emotional awareness. You'd be like a ship adrift, tossed about by unpredictable emotional storms. Emotional awareness provides us with the map and guidance we need to navigate these waters with confidence and clarity.

The journey of personal growth is intricately connected to emotional awareness. It's through this awareness that we gain insights into our thought patterns, triggers, and behaviours. For instance, if you experience a surge of anger during a work meeting, emotional awareness prompts you to inquire about the source of this anger. Is it a feeling of being dismissed? Is it linked to an unmet expectation? By dissecting the emotional response, you gain the power to address its underlying cause, paving the way for growth and transformation.

One of the wondrous byproducts of emotional awareness is empathy, the ability to understand and share the feelings of others. When we recognize and comprehend our own emotions, we develop a foundation that enables us to step into the shoes of those around us. This bridge of empathy connects us on a human level, fostering deeper connections and more meaningful relationships.

Imagine a world where empathy flourishes, where misunderstandings are replaced by understanding, and judgment transforms into compassion. Emotional awareness serves as the cornerstone of this world, a world that recognizes the universality of human emotions and the power of shared experience.

Now, let's explore how emotional intelligence fits into this tapestry.

What is? Emotional intelligence is the ability to recognize, understand, manage, and effectively utilize our emotions and those of others. It involves empathy, self-awareness, and self-regulation. In a world filled with emojis and acronyms, it's easy to overlook the nuances that constitute emotional intelligence. This emotional radar allows us to navigate the complex landscape of human interaction.

Confidence, a close companion of emotional intelligence, plays a pivotal role in its development. Confidence is the gentle hand that pulls you out of your emotional comfort zone. When you're confident, you're more willing to embrace vulnerability, take emotional risks, and engage in genuine conversations. In essence, confidence helps you navigate the turbulent waters of human emotion with greater finesse.

Oddly, some people channel their emotional intelligence into physical pursuits. The gym becomes a sanctuary for releasing emotional tension. Lifting weights, running, or cycling offers an avenue to channel emotional energy into physical progress. While physical pain doesn't necessarily equate to emotional growth, it's one way some people cope. We sweat out our anxieties, ultimately building confidence.

In our world, communication is vital, but the fear of revealing our true selves can hold us back. By nurturing emotional intelligence, we not only learn more about ourselves but also about the people we interact with. It's not about trying to be someone else but rather a process of self-reflection and self-improvement. Without it, we're like a fish trying to dance on a wet floor – awkward and out of sync.

The Divine Psychological Journey

Fig:, †

Out of one`s element

As we navigate the intricate dance between our thoughts and feelings, emotional awareness guides us through uncharted territories, revealing insights that foster growth, connection, and resilience. It invites us to embrace vulnerability, to recognize that emotions are not to be feared but to be acknowledged and understood. Navigate the twists and turns of trust, fear, and vulnerability, we'll find that self-awareness and confidence are the keys to unlocking the hidden halls of emotional intelligence.

Speaking of emotional intelligence, have you ever noticed how good jokes can lift your mood? Laughter is a secret doorway to emotional understanding. Find the humour in life, and you'll unlock even more of your emotional intelligence.

Time to lift your MOOD NOW: Why did the emotionally intelligent person bring a dumbbell to the gym? Because they wanted to work out their empathy muscles, lifting the weight of understanding one emotion at a time! LOL

On a more serious note, emotional intelligence isn't just a buzzword; it's a powerful force that can shape the course of our relationships. As I dive into the realms of emotional intelligence, I begin to see the profound influence it wields over our connections with others. In those moments where my emotional intelligence faltered, I struggled to connect, empathize, and, admittedly, I made some regrettable decisions. (Sorry, friends. We all have our moments, right?)

In life, we encounter a multitude of personalities, each on a unique and fascinating journey. But here's the kicker, folks – when it comes to our intimate relationships, emotional intelligence can make or break the deal.

Let's dive a bit deeper into this.

When emotional intelligence is lacking in a couple's relationship, it's alike to navigating a ship through treacherous waters without a compass. The essence of emotional intelligence lies in recognizing, understanding, and managing emotions, both within us and in others. It's about empathizing, communicating, and connecting on a profound level. So, when emotional intelligence is absent from the equation, it can lead to misunderstandings, miscommunications, and emotional discord.

Picture this: your partner expresses frustration after a long, tough day at work. Without emotional intelligence, you might misinterpret their irritation as directed at you, leading to an argument that could have been avoided. Or perhaps your emotional responses are excessive, causing unnecessary strain in your relationship. These are the psychological reasons behind the destructive impact of low emotional intelligence.

Therefore, emotional intelligence fundamentally influences how we understand, express, and manage emotions, both in ourselves and in others. When we lack emotional intelligence, we struggle to comprehend our own feelings, let alone those of our partner.

How do I manage my emotional radar?

First, I created a cozy, comforting space in my room. Then, I bought a stars and nebula projector to cast mesmerizing cosmic scenes on my ceiling - **Yes, I know what you're thinking, crazy!** But this setup helps me relax and engage in introspection.

I'd lie down, relax, and just have an open conversation with myself. This isn't a monologue; it`s a dialogue. I ask myself those "mighty questions", I'd review my day, pondering my reactions when I felt anger or frustration. Was I right in those moments? Why did I feel the way I did? The cornerstone of this process is asking yourself 'why.' Just like a professional therapist might ask.

Alongside 'why,' there's the crucial question – 'how did it make you feel?'

It's not about trying to be someone else or overthinking every interaction. Instead, it's a process of self-reflection and self-improvement.

By asking these questions, I can embark on a journey of self-discovery, introspection, and self-improvement. Challenge myself to be a better person, a better partner, and a kinder soul. In the end, our mission is simple – be nicer to the world and the people we share it with.

In the grand narrative of life, none of us are flawless characters. We each have our unique quirks, our personal journeys of self-discovery, and our own quests to enhance emotional intelligence. It's all part of the wonderfully messy and intricate tapestry of existence.

But here's the reassuring truth - Imperfections and emotions are what make us human. Our emotions, with all their complexities and subtleties, are the colours that paint the vivid portrait of our lives. Each day offers us opportunities to learn, to reflect, and to be a little better than we were yesterday.

We each have our unique quirks, our personal journeys of self-discovery, and our own quests to enhance emotional intelligence. It's all part of the wonderfully messy and intricate tapestry of existence.

So, let's be proud of our imperfections, our emotions, and the journey we're on. There's no endpoint, no ultimate perfection to achieve - there's just the beautiful evolution of the self.

Here's to embracing the journey, one question, one reflection, and one starry night at a time. After all, in the grand cosmos of existence, we are the brightest stars, imperfections and all.

Online/Offline

Chapter 2-

IMPORTANCE OF ONLINE INTELLIGENCE

Welcome to the fascinating world of Emotional and Online Intelligence, an electrifying duo poised to redefine your journey through the digital realm while elevating your human connections.

In the previous chapter, we ventured into the depths of emotional awareness, unravelling the profound impact it can have on our lives. Now, we're poised to explore the captivating domain of Online Intelligence, and, together, we'll uncover the importance of marrying these two skills for a deeper comprehension of ourselves and those we encounter.

#playmusic

In today's fast-paced world, the digital landscape is as crucial to our daily lives as the air we breathe.

With social media, emails, and messaging apps permeating our existence, we're more interconnected than ever before.

This interconnectedness serves as the conduit for our thoughts and emotions, frequently shared with the entire world.

Yet, as we engage in this digital dance, it's imperative that we do so with a heightened level of awareness.

Much like a choreographed dance, where every step contributes to the grand performance, our online presence has a profound impact on the digital community. Imagine your online interactions as your unique dance moves in this grand ballroom of connectivity. Each move creates a rhythm, shaping the essence of the digital world. Before you elegantly waltz your thoughts onto the online dance floor, pause for a moment to consider their potential impact. Just as you wouldn't want to misstep on the toes of your dance partner, you want to ensure your digital presence aligns with your values and emotional awareness.

We are now in an era where emotional intelligence and online intelligence are intricately connected, complementing each other like Batman and Robin, working in tandem to elevate our interactions, whether in-person or online.

This interconnectedness offers a new perspective: the more you refine your emotional intelligence, the more attuned you become to the emotions that underpin your online engagements. As you scroll through your social media feed, you'll be more conscious of the emotions that drive these interactions.

Your digital footprint takes on a more mindful tone, as your online presence harmonizes with your values and emotional awareness.

In this digital age, it's not uncommon to be inundated with seemingly flawless lives, picture-perfect moments, and #LifeGoals. But beneath these polished exteriors, there exist unique and authentic stories, often yearning to be told. We're caught in the race to portray an idealized version of ourselves, neatly tucking our struggles behind filters. However, under the facade, we each bear a distinctive narrative waiting to be shared. It's high time we embrace these genuine stories, understanding that each is a piece of the larger human mosaic.

Here's where Online Intelligence becomes our guiding star. It encourages us to pause and reflect on the emotions underlying these seemingly perfect narratives. What fears, concerns, or misunderstandings drive these seemingly perfect online lives? By practicing Online Intelligence, we transform ourselves into digital peacemakers, nurturing a more compassionate and productive online environment.

Online platforms become our confessional, inviting us to share our emotional struggles, often with a veil of anonymity that assures solace and understanding.

Yet, the digital realm is replete with contradictions.

While it offers empathy and support, it also harbours misinformation and distorted perspectives. Sharing your innermost thoughts on an online forum about, say, depression, may yield responses filled with advice and camaraderie. But alongside the guiding stars, there exists the potential for misguided counsel and skewed perspectives. The path to healing is not one-size-fits-all; it is a journey filled with compassion and potential pitfalls.

Finding the delicate balance between Emotional Intelligence and Online Intelligence is the key.

Spending too much time online can lead to emotional detachment, while permitting digital interactions to negatively impact your emotions is equally undesirable. Striking this balance is essential, as it empowers you to be more aware of how your online presence influences your emotional state.

Understanding the types of content that trigger specific emotions or recognizing the individuals who consistently elicit varied emotional responses, can significantly enhance your digital well-being.

The ability to decipher these complexities, fathom our emotions, and empathize with others forms the core of Online Intelligence.

In this grand online dance, choosing your battles wisely and reflecting upon your digital footprints are steps in cultivating your Online Intelligence. Each interaction, post, or comment you make contributes to the symphony of the internet, leaving a distinct imprint. As we conclude this chapter, remember that the practice of Online Intelligence is a skill that can be developed and polished over time.

But our journey doesn't stop here. The interplay between online intelligence and emotional intelligence is at the heart of the matter, and we'll delve deeper into this symbiotic relationship in the forthcoming chapters. I've ventured out of my comfort zone to immerse myself in various, sometimes challenging, online situations, all in pursuit of uncovering how these two intelligences intertwine to craft a richer and more enlightening digital experience. Stay tuned, for there is much more to discover in the chapters that lie ahead.

The Divine Psychological Journey

Illustration of navigating between emotional and online Colosseum

Fig ≥ fig

The Divine Psychological Journey

My favourite chapter.

Chapter 3-

THE MAIN CHARACTER SYNDROME

In the age of social media, our lives have undergone a transformation of epic proportions. With the tap of a screen, we can share our thoughts, experiences, and even our daily routines with the world. It's an era where we all have the opportunity to be the main character in our own digital story. But what lies beneath this desire for the spotlight and the virtual applause? Is it the pursuit of online affection and affirmation that fuels this digital drama?

In recent years, it's become increasingly evident how social media platforms have influenced and, in some ways, changed the very fabric of our humanity. The allure of online affection has led us down a path where validation is measured in likes, comments, and the coveted "tap taps." We engage in a myriad of online activities, from posting videos and duets to going live, all in the relentless pursuit of affirmation.

But what psychological forces drive this quest for online approval?

Social Validation: Psychologically, the need for social validation is deeply ingrained in our nature. It's a fundamental human desire to be acknowledged and accepted by our peers. Social media platforms tap into this by offering instant feedback and recognition.

Comparison and Insecurity: The scrolling culture of social media exposes us to countless "perfect" lives, carefully curated and filtered. As we compare ourselves to these idealized versions, feelings of insecurity and inadequacy creep in. To compensate, we seek validation online, hoping to bridge the gap between our real selves and the personas we encounter online.

Dopamine Rush: Every like, comment, or share triggers a release of dopamine in our brains, the pleasure-seeking neurotransmitter. This creates a feedback loop where we yearn for more online affection to experience that rush again, much like a gambler seeking another win
Amid this digital quest for affirmation, concerns arise about the potential impact on real-life human interaction.

HOWEVER,

Paradoxically, even as we accumulate online affection, real-life loneliness is on the rise. The more likes we gather, the emptier we seem to feel. But why?

This phenomenon, often referred to as the "loneliness paradox," is grounded in psychological research and it appears that online connections often remain superficial. We may have hundreds of "friends" and "followers," but how many of them truly know us? The paradox lies in the shallowness of these connections compared to the deep yearning for genuine human interaction.

The digital realm allows us to craft a carefully curated image, hiding our vulnerabilities and flaws. This fear of revealing our true selves can hinder authentic relationships. We become locked in our self-created characters, afraid of exposing our human imperfections.

Our obsession with comparing ourselves to others, fuelled by online content, can lead to feelings of isolation. We perceive others as happier, more successful, or more popular, further distancing ourselves from genuine connections.

Let's diagnose this.

> "The main Character Syndrome"

"The Main Character Syndrome." I want to describe it as a condition where the constant online validation convinces us that we are the protagonists of our own stories, each one more important than the last.

As this syndrome takes hold, we begin to see ourselves as central figures, increasingly detached from the reality of our lives. We start to believe that we are the main characters in a world where everyone else is just an extra.

Like a hiding place. Much like choosing video game characters to escape reality as children, this syndrome becomes a hiding place. It allows us to play a character that hides our true selves behind a mask of online perfection, reinforcing our self-denial.

This syndrome tricks us into thinking we are more powerful, important, and clever than others, echoing the behaviour of celebrities who may deny their true selves out of fear.

The Divine Psychological Journey

But why do we yearn for this alternate character? At its core, it often boils down to our insecurities. Social media exposes us to countless seemingly "perfect" lives, and our brains can struggle to reconcile this idealized reality with our own. In response, the brain simulates an alternate identity—the main character—who stands on equal footing or even surpasses these online idols.

This character serves as a shield against our insecurities, allowing us to momentarily escape our own reality. However, the danger lies in mistaking this character for our true selves, leading to a disconnect between who we are online and who we are in the real world.

It's crucial to remember that behind every screen lies a real person, vulnerabilities, imperfections, and all. The quest for online validation can be a never-ending loop, leaving us feeling lonelier than ever.

The true remedy lies in embracing our authenticity, accepting our imperfections, and seeking genuine connections beyond the digital veil. The digital world can be a place of affirmation, but it should never replace the richness of real-life human interaction. Let us not forget that, in the grand story of our lives, we are not just the main character but part of an ensemble cast, each with a unique role to play in creating meaningful connections and authentic relationships.

The Divine Psychological Journey

The main Character

Fig   ©

My algorithm it's so confused.

Chapter 4-

THE SOCIAL MEDIA EXPERIMENT: EXPLORING THE IMPACT ON WELL-BEING

Over the past three years, I embarked on a personal experiment with social media, intentionally going on and off these platforms to observe the effects on my well-being. This experiment allowed me to understand how social media influences my emotions and behaviours, particularly by manipulating the content I engage with and the algorithms that shape my online experience. Let's delve into my journey and the psychological reasons behind the different topics I chose to explore.

The Divine Psychological Journey

Either I grow with you, or I outgrow you.

Fig.,3

Spending less time on social media, I feel less distracted and more energized.

During the periods when I stayed away from social media, I noticed a significant decrease in the time spent on my phone. This newfound freedom from constant scrolling allowed me to focus on daily tasks, ultimately leading to a sense of accomplishment and productivity. I felt less distracted and more present in the moment, enabling me to fully engage with real-life experiences.

However, it's important to acknowledge that while distancing myself from social media provided these benefits, I also experienced a sense of disconnection and detachment from the online world. Social media has become deeply ingrained in our lives, and despite its downsides, it serves as a means of connection, staying informed, and even self-expression.

During my forays into social media, I deliberately chose to engage with various topics, each evoking unique emotional response. These experiences shed light on the psychological reasons behind my emotional reactions.

Let's explore a few examples:

1 Car Accidents Videos: Paranoia and Nightmares

Engaging with videos depicting car accidents triggered intense feelings of paranoia and anxiety while driving. The vivid imagery of crashes and potential harm created a heightened sense of vulnerability. I found myself constantly looking over my shoulder, anticipating danger on the road even when there was no immediate threat. This heightened state of alertness, while intended to promote safety, became a source of distress and anxiety.

These feelings didn't just stay confined to my waking hours. They infiltrated my dreams, manifesting as nightmares where I would find myself involved in horrific car accidents. These nightmares intensified the underlying fear and paranoia, leaving me feeling unsettled even during sleep.

The psychological reason behind this response lies in our brain's ability to internalize and replay distressing images. When we repeatedly expose ourselves to traumatic or fear-inducing content, it can heighten our perception of danger and trigger a chronic state of anxiety. The mind becomes hyper-vigilant, constantly on the lookout for potential threats, even in situations where they may be unlikely.

2 Sad and Depressing Quotes: Worthlessness and Loneliness

Reading sad and depressing quotes on social media had a profound impact on my emotional state, evoking feelings of worthlessness and deep sadness. The constant exposure to such content reinforced negative thought patterns, amplifying self-doubt and self-criticism. These quotes resonated with my own insecurities and vulnerabilities, magnifying my perceived flaws and shortcomings.

As I scrolled through these quotes, a sense of loneliness engulfed me. The raw emotions expressed in the words of others made me feel like I was not alone in my pain, but it also intensified my own feelings of isolation. It seemed as though everyone else understood this deep sense of despair, while I felt left behind, disconnected from a collective understanding.

The psychological reason behind this response lies in the brain's tendency to latch onto negative stimuli. Our brains are wired to pay more attention to negative information as a means of self-protection. This negativity bias can lead to a heightened sensitivity to sad or depressing content, reinforcing negative emotions and thoughts. Additionally, the feelings of loneliness may stem from a sense of social comparison, where we perceive others as more connected and understood, exacerbating our own feelings of isolation.

3 Dogs and Animals: Mood Elevation and Increased Online Engagement

Engaging with content related to dogs and animals had a profound effect on my mood, eliciting feelings of joy, companionship, and warmth. The sight of a cute puppy or heartwarming animal rescue story would bring a smile to my face and a sense of happiness. These images tapped into our inherent connection with nature and our desire for love and companionship.

However, this positive emotional response came with a downside. The captivating nature of these posts led me to spend more time online, scrolling through endless pictures and videos of adorable animals. What started as a momentary mood booster turned into a distraction that consumed more of my time and attention than I had intended.

The psychological reason behind this response lies in the brain's reward system. When we encounter pleasant and engaging stimuli, such as cute animal images, our brain releases feel-good neurotransmitters like dopamine. This creates a positive reinforcement loop, encouraging us to seek out more of these experiences. However, this can also lead to excessive online engagement and a potential neglect of real-life responsibilities.

4 Different Memes: Uncontrollable Creativity and Varied Ideas

Engaging with different memes sparked a surge of creativity within me. The clever wordplay, humorous images, and unexpected juxtapositions triggered a stream of new ideas and unconventional perspectives. Each meme served as a catalyst for creative thinking, prompting me to explore different angles and connections.

However, this influx of ideas sometimes became overwhelming. It was as if my mind was racing in multiple directions, making it difficult to focus on a single task or train of thought. The constant influx of memes and their contagious nature led me down a rabbit hole of inspiration, but it also posed challenges in maintaining a structured and focused mindset.

The psychological reason behind this response lies in the brain's ability to generate connections and associations. Memes often rely on unexpected and novel juxtapositions, triggering our brain's natural inclination to find patterns and make connections. While this can stimulate creative thinking, it can also lead to a scattered and unfocused mind, as we become bombarded with an abundance of ideas and possibilities.

Understanding these psychological factors allows us to make more conscious choices about the content we engage with on social media. It highlights the importance of being mindful of the emotional impact and recognizing the potential risks and benefits associated with different topics. By being aware of these influences, we can curate our online experiences to better support our mental well-being.

Additionally, I became increasingly concerned about the psychological reasons behind our brain's reactions to the ever-evolving landscape of social media. With the massive number of views and interactions happening online, I couldn't help but wonder why we are so captivated by certain elements, such as having someone's podcast playing at the top of the screen while simultaneously watching someone play a game at the bottom.

One possible explanation for this engagement is the concept of novelty and multisensory stimulation. Our brains are wired to seek out new and interesting experiences, and the combination of visual and auditory stimuli in this format provides a unique and engaging sensory experience. The simultaneous presence of different forms of content taps into our inherent curiosity, keeping us hooked and wanting more.

Furthermore, the presence of poorly played video game ads caught my attention. It seemed counterintuitive to showcase someone performing poorly in a video game, yet it held my attention. This phenomenon can be attributed to the psychological concept of "the curiosity gap." By showing suboptimal gameplay, advertisers create a sense of curiosity and anticipation in viewers. Our brains crave closure and resolution, driving us to engage with the content in hopes of uncovering a solution or improvement.

The integration of video game elements and distractions within social media platforms taps into our innate desire for novelty, multisensory experiences, and closure. These psychological mechanisms, combined with the addictive nature of social media, create an environment where users are compelled to stay engaged, often at the expense of our attention and time.

Anyway, behold the marvellous world of the digital realm, where our behaviours and perceptions are under the whimsical spell of psychological influences! But fear not, my fellow cyber wanderers, for with knowledge comes power, and we shall uncover the secrets of social media platforms and advertisers!

By embracing our newfound awareness, we can bravely make informed choices about our digital escapades and set boundaries to protect our precious mental well-being. Oh, yes, we shall question the motives behind the design and content we consume, avoiding the treacherous pitfalls of mindless distraction!

The Divine Psychological Journey

You see, my friends, it's all about maintaining that sense of agency and control over our online adventures. Understanding the psychological reasons behind our digital dance allows us to navigate the enchanted landscape of social media with our eyes wide open! We shall align our choices with our values and well-being, forging a path of wisdom and whimsy in this vast digital wonderland!

So, let us venture forth with a twinkle in our eyes and a giggle in our hearts as we bravely embrace the magical journey of digital exploration! Onward, my cyber companions, to a world where knowledge reigns supreme, and our well-being shall flourish in the realm of social media!

If there is delusion there is hope…

Chapter 5-

NAVIGATING THE LABYRINTH: MODERN DATING

As a single man in the modern world, my dating experiences have been diverse and enlightening, serving as a rich tapestry of emotional learning and personal growth. They have taught me about human nature, about the complexities of emotions, and perhaps most importantly, about myself.

One of the first things that stood out to me during my dating experiences was the incredible diversity of people and personalities out there. Each woman I've had the chance to get to know has been unique in her own way, with her distinct set of interests, quirks, and life experiences.

The world of dating has also brought to the fore the complex dance between emotional and logical decision-making. There are instances when emotions run high, passion obscures reason, and the heart seems to have a mind of its own.

On the other hand, there are times when logic dictates, questioning the viability of a potential relationship based on practical considerations.

NOTE TO SELF - I've learned that while the heart's impulses shouldn't be ignored, they also shouldn't completely overshadow logic. Balance, as with many things in life, seems to be the key.

Let's talk about online dating. And what I found out whilst trying to date online.

The Divine Psychological Journey

An illustration of my online dating experience.

Fig., π

As we delve into the perplexing world of modern dating, I must confess my dislike for the notion of online dating. Let me make my case: The more options we have at our fingertips, the less we tend to invest in what we already possess. It's a psychological trap that lures us into a cycle of perpetual indecision and emotional detachment.

Imagine this: You're strolling through a bountiful garden, where every flower represents a potential romantic connection. Online dating platforms provide a seemingly endless array of flowers, all vying for our attention. With each new option, our investment in any individual dwindles. Why commit when there's always another potential match just a swipe away?

This phenomenon can be attributed to the "Paradox of Choice," a psychological concept that suggests an abundance of options can lead to decision paralysis and a decrease in overall satisfaction. When we have numerous possibilities, we become consumed by the fear of making the wrong choice. Consequently, we invest less emotionally, keeping one foot perpetually out the door.

Allow me to present an alternative perspective. Imagine a different scenario: You meet someone in an organic, face-to-face encounter, where the dance of conversation and shared experiences unfolds naturally. In this scenario, the investment is higher from the start. You invest time, energy, and emotions into fostering a connection with a singular individual.

Psychologically speaking, investing in a single option fosters a deeper sense of commitment and attachment. This investment activates our innate need for connection and intimacy. By focusing on one person, we allow ourselves to truly explore and understand the intricacies of that individual, forming a foundation for a potentially meaningful and fulfilling relationship.

But why, then, does online dating continue to flourish? What draws people to this realm of seemingly endless choices? The answer lies in several psychological factors that make online dating appealing.

Firstly, the allure of online dating stems from the convenience and accessibility it offers. In a fast-paced world where time is a precious commodity, these platforms provide a quick and efficient means of meeting potential partners.

The ease of swiping and matching taps into our desire for instant gratification and the possibility of finding a compatible match without investing significant effort.

Secondly, online dating satisfies our innate curiosity. Humans are naturally curious beings, and the vast array of profiles becomes a tantalizing playground for exploration. We're enticed by the prospect of discovering new personalities, shared interests, and potential chemistry, all at our fingertips.

Lastly, online dating can also serve as a buffer against potential rejection. The digital realm offers a certain level of anonymity and distance, shielding us from face-to-face rejection. It provides a perceived sense of control, allowing individuals to carefully craft their online persona and present an idealized version of themselves. But let's talk about the psychological aspect of it.

Psychological Explanation: Fear of Missing Out (FOMO) and Commitment Avoidance

In the fast-paced world of modern dating, the fear of missing out (FOMO) can cast a shadow over the development of deep and meaningful connections. As humans, we naturally seek novelty, excitement, and the potential for new experiences.

With online dating offering an abundance of options, individuals often find themselves torn between committing to one person and the enticing possibility of something better just around the corner.

FOMO takes root when individuals become preoccupied with the idea that by committing to a single partner, they may be closing the door on other potentially rewarding connections. The constant access to an ever-expanding pool of potential partners intensifies this fear. Thoughts like "What if someone better comes along?" or "What if I'm missing out on a more compatible match?" become common in the minds of those plagued by FOMO.

This fear creates a sense of commitment avoidance, where individuals hesitate to invest fully in a relationship. They may hold back emotionally, subconsciously reserving a part of themselves for the possibility of someone new entering their lives. Commitment avoidance can manifest as maintaining emotional distance, avoiding conversations about the future, or perpetually seeking the thrill of the chase rather than cultivating a deeper connection.

Another psychological factor that contributes to reduced investment is the concept of "choice overload." When faced with a multitude of options, individuals can feel overwhelmed and paralyzed by the decision-making process. The belief that there is an endless array of alternatives can lead to a lack of commitment or a perpetual state of indecision.

With so many choices available, individuals may struggle to settle on a single person, fearing that they may be making the wrong decision or prematurely closing themselves off from other possibilities.

Ultimately, the fear of missing out and the burden of choice overload hinder individuals from investing wholeheartedly in a relationship. It becomes difficult to fully engage, trust, and nurture a connection when the mind is fixated on what might lie beyond the current partnership. Overcoming these psychological barriers requires introspection, self-awareness, and a conscious effort to recognize the value of commitment and the rewards that come with investing deeply in a relationship.

However, as alluring as online dating may be, we must recognize its potential pitfalls. The allure of choice can diminish our investment in a single person, hindering the development of meaningful connections.

Moreover, the lack of nonverbal cues in online communication can lead to misinterpretation, misunderstandings, and a false sense of intimacy.

So, dear reader, as we navigate the labyrinth of modern dating, let us approach it with caution. Let us be mindful of the psychological implications of an excess of options, and the potential consequences of investing less and less in the connections we forge. Perhaps, by recognizing the value of investing in a single option and embracing the vulnerability that comes with it, we can uncover the true depths of meaningful relationships in this complex digital age.

Remember, the choices we make in our pursuit of love and connection shape our experiences. Choose wisely, invest wholeheartedly, and may you find the profound and genuine connections you seek in this ever-evolving landscape of modern dating.

Let me share with you the psychological challenges I encountered and how they affected my self-perception and emotional well-being. It's been quite a journey, and I've learned some valuable lessons along the way.

Case Study: Alex - The Struggle with Online Dating

Name: Alex

Age: 26

As a 26-year-old navigating the world of online dating, I found myself facing a series of challenges that impacted my self-perception and emotional well-being. The frustrations of receiving few matches and likes on dating platforms, coupled with unsuccessful connections and forced interactions, led to feelings of insecurity, self-doubt, and a sense of being incapable of forming genuine connections.

Psychological Factors: Overwhelming Insecurity and Self-Doubt and its Impact on Self-Worth

The overwhelming insecurity and self-doubt that I experienced through online dating had a profound effect on my own sense of worth. Each instance of rejection or lack of interest felt like a personal rejection of my entire being. It became difficult to separate the lack of matches and likes from my own value as an individual.

The constant exposure to seemingly perfect profiles and comparisons to others only intensified my feelings of inadequacy. It felt as though I was constantly falling short of the societal ideals and expectations set by online dating platforms. I started questioning my physical attractiveness, my personality, and my worthiness of love and connection.

These negative self-perceptions began to seep into other areas of my life as well. I found myself doubting my capabilities and second-guessing my worth in various aspects, not just in the context of online dating. The impact of these feelings of unworthiness extended far beyond the digital realm, affecting my confidence, self-esteem, and overall well-being.

The constant cycle of self-doubt and questioning eroded my self-image, leaving me feeling trapped in a negative narrative about myself. It became challenging to see my own strengths and positive qualities, as my focus was fixated on the perceived flaws and shortcomings that I believed made me unworthy of love and connection.

Over time, it became clear that my worth as an individual should not be tied solely to external validation through online dating.

The Divine Psychological Journey

I began to realize that my value was not determined by the number of matches or likes I received, but by the inherent qualities, uniqueness, and strengths that I possessed as a person.

In order to rebuild my self-worth, I embarked on a journey of self-discovery and self-acceptance. I sought to identify and appreciate my own strengths, passions, and values, independent of the judgments and expectations of others. This process involved practicing self-compassion, challenging negative self-talk, and fostering a positive mindset that focused on my worthiness of love and connection regardless of online dating outcomes.

While the impact on my self-worth was significant, I also recognized that it was within my power to redefine my own value and regain a sense of self-worth that was not contingent upon external validation. Through self-reflection, personal growth, and a shift in perspective, I began to embrace my worthiness of love and connection.

from a place of authenticity and self-acceptance.

Engaging in conversations with individuals I met through online dating often left me feeling dissatisfied and disconnected. The pressure to impress and the expectation of finding an instant connection often resulted in interactions that felt forced or inauthentic. It seemed as though the conversations lacked depth, genuine interest, and a natural flow.

This disconnect contributed to feelings of frustration and disappointment.

I questioned whether the problem lay with me or with the nature of online dating itself. The constant effort to maintain engaging conversations and the lack of reciprocation from the other person left me feeling emotionally drained and discouraged.

While the challenges of online dating took a toll on my self-esteem, they also provided an opportunity for personal growth and resilience. Through self-reflection, I began to recognize that the online dating experience was not a reflection of my worth as an individual. I realized that the limited number of matches and unsuccessful connections were not indicative of my value or desirability.

By reframing my mindset, I developed a more resilient outlook. Instead of viewing each interaction as a personal judgment, I started seeing them as learning experiences. I began to focus on qualities beyond physical appearance and external validation, valuing authenticity and genuine connections over superficial indicators of interest.

These differences have sometimes been a source of confusion or conflict, as I've grappled with understanding viewpoints that diverged from my own. But they've also been a wellspring of growth, pushing me to broaden my horizons and develop a more open, understanding mindset.

Counterarguments or Debates?

Chapter 6-

THE DATING AND ITS EVOLUTIONARY PSYCHOLOGY

Ladies and gentlemen, gather 'round for a journey that'll tickle your brain cells and might even make you question your dating game. That's right, we're diving into the mesmerizing world of dating, guided by the whimsical hand of evolutionary psychology. Let's think about it – the awkward first dates, the fluttery stomach, and the eternal struggle to figure out who should text first. Oh, the joys of the dating dance! Join us as we waltz through the fascinating interplay between our ancestral instincts and the modern dating landscape.

The Evolutionary Groove:

Picture this: our caveman and cavewoman ancestors, armed with spears and animal hides, navigating the prehistoric realm. In those ancient days, courtship was less about swiping right and more about providing resources like food, shelter, and protection. Survival was on the menu, and our ancestors knew how to serve it hot. It's like they were playing the ultimate long game – ensuring their genes had the best shot at survival.

The Divine Psychological Journey

DNA groove

Fig 88

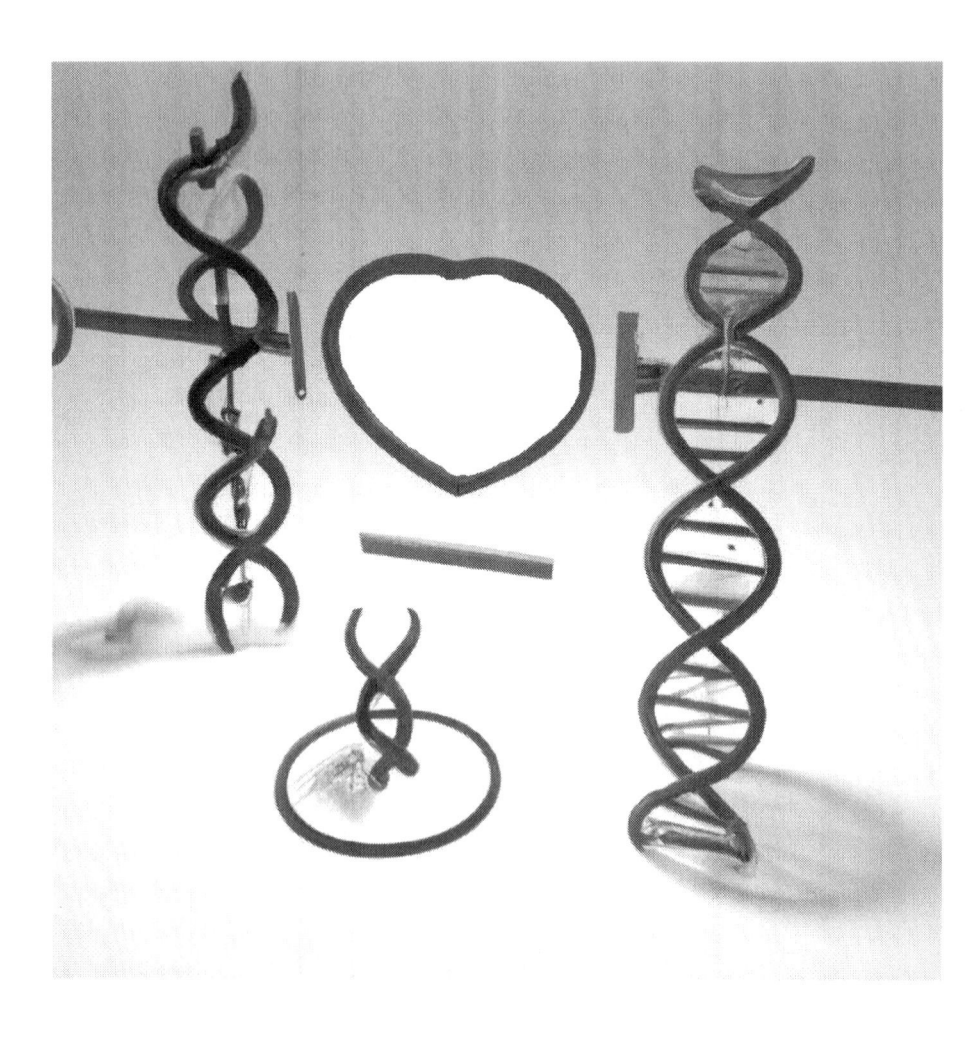

The Divine Psychological Journey

But did we discover love through survival, or did we survive because of love?

What came first, the egg or the chicken? Love or survival?

But what is love? Some would say that love is a chemistry where our bodies and brains release some 'love toxins,' and we fall in love chemically. Others say that love is something given to you by a divine hand, or that love is written in the thread of life. Clearly, the answer to this question is highly subjective. You see, I believe we are who we are due to the experiences and decisions we make in life. Is it important to learn from mistakes?

I believe that 'love' is a manifestation of a person different from yourself. It is a reflection of a person on our lives. We all expect a prince or princess to come on a white horse or in a carriage. And whether we admit it or not, this manifestation we create involuntarily is very limited, and the list of 'rules' increases with each experience.

Love, in my view, is that person you manifested and fulfills each 'rule' you have.

Where and how do the separations occur? Well, as I said at the beginning, the manifestation is very restricted. Usually, you only think about the positive aspects of that person, but being human, we have 'flawed qualities' too. These flawed qualities are perfectly normal.

Some people don't eat as we would like them to, they are not as clean and organized as we would like, and every flawed quality you present, your brain perceives it to tell you: actually, it's not what you manifested.

Confusing.

When you manifest a person, make sure you manifest those flawed qualities too. And you have flawed qualities; you must be prepared to let go of, in addition to hair color and height, where to throw your sock, when to brush your teeth, and how to chew - maybe then the right person will manifest to you. Now don't just focus on the flawed qualities, be positive, I say just be attentive to what you desire.

But what is the correct path in life? I don't believe there is that 'correct path,' because sometimes even the wrong path is the 'correct path.'

A question I asked myself after breakups was, 'Did I love myself enough for the other person to love me as much as I loved myself?'

It hurts, but it works, at least for me.

We've deviated from the subject, apologies, I have an evening with wiser and surprisingly sad thinking.

NOTE TO MYSELF: No regrets because I know that my heart was pure.

The Divine Psychological Journey

Our ancestral instincts, forged in the crucible of survival, were fundamental to the relationships of our cave-dwelling forebears. These instincts revolved around procreation, protection, and resource-sharing. In the harsh environment of early humanity, men often assumed the role of protectors and providers, while women prioritized selecting mates who could offer security and resources. These ancestral patterns laid the foundation for how we approach romantic relationships today, with echoes of these instincts often influencing our preferences and desires.

Now, consider the possibility of divine influence in these ancient dynamics. Could it be that our ancestors, driven by these survival instincts, were also guided by divine whispers directing them towards partners with whom they would embark on profound spiritual journeys? In this interpretation, the choices made by our ancestors weren't solely driven by earthly desires but were part of a grander plan, orchestrated by divine forces to aid not only in survival but also in the growth of the human spirit.

The Divine Psychological Journey

Psychologically, we can understand these ancestral instincts through the lens of evolutionary psychology. These instincts were advantageous in an environment where survival was challenging. Modern research in psychology reveals how these ancient patterns continue to influence our mate preferences, attachment styles, and even the emotions we experience in relationships. For example, our attachment styles, shaped by early caregiver relationships, often mirror the dynamics of trust, dependence, and intimacy seen in ancestral pair bonding.

The interplay between these elements becomes truly captivating when we acknowledge that our psychological patterns, influenced by ancestral instincts, might also be guided or influenced by divine forces. In this complex tapestry, our romantic choices and emotional attachments can be viewed as a blend of biology, psychology, and spiritual guidance. The pursuit of love, once seen as a product of ancestral survival mechanisms, takes on a more profound dimension, where each relationship may hold the potential for both personal growth and a deeper connection with the divine.

In essence, the connections between ancestral instincts, cave man-woman relationships, divine feelings, and psychological explanations form a rich tapestry that shapes our romantic lives. This interplay reflects the intricate dance of our past, our beliefs, and the very essence of what it means to be human.

Fast-forward to the present, where swanky cars and luxury watches have become the new currency of courtship. Men, driven by a subconscious whisper from their ancestors, believe that these flashy possessions signal their ability to provide for a potential partner. But hold on – the script has been flipped! Women are rising, claiming their throne of independence. The allure of traditional displays of wealth is losing its sparkle, as equality paints a new landscape of connection based on shared dreams and values.

In the enigmatic world of modern dating, the interplay between evolutionary psychology, divine guidance, and contemporary intricacies creates a tapestry of complexities that define our romantic pursuits. It's a journey where ancient instincts, carefully woven into our DNA by eons of evolution, meet the subtle whispers of divine guidance, shaping the choices we make in our quest for love and connection.

The Divine Psychological Journey

Our ancestral instincts, honed through countless generations, have left an indelible mark on the dynamics of contemporary relationships. These instincts, rooted in survival and procreation, continue to influence our dating preferences. Yet, in this intricate dance, there's a question that lingers – could there be more to our choices than mere biology? Are spiritual forces at play, gently nudging us towards partners with whom we share not only our earthly desires but also a deeper spiritual journey?

The Dance of Attraction and Protection:

Let's cha-cha our way to the next act – the dance of attraction and protection. Imagine this dance floor: men flexing their muscles to showcase their protective prowess, and women enhancing their charm to communicate fertility and health. It's like a cosmic biology class with a dash of flirtation. But hang on – the dance card has changed! Society's script now includes empowerment, and women are demanding emotional resonance over old-school protection.

Dodging the Dance Steps:

But oh, the dance floor isn't just glitter and glamour. The intricate steps of evolutionary psychology entwine with the rapidly changing rhythms of society, creating a dance that's part foxtrot, part hip-hop. Men, feeling a tad lost in this new choreography, might be left wondering, "Do I pay for dinner, or is that outdated now?" The tango between age-old instincts and the evolving dance of dating can leave anyone's head spinning faster than a Beyoncé dance break.

Emotional Pas de Deux:

Amidst the twirls and spins, let's spotlight emotional attachment. Childhood experiences, like little choreographers, shape our adult dance moves. Those who waltzed through childhood with emotional security might find the adult dance smooth, while those whose early years were more like a chaotic mosh pit might struggle with the intricate waltz of intimacy.

Rewriting the Choreography:

Navigating the labyrinth of emotional attachment in the context of modern dating is like deciphering a complex riddle. Childhood experiences, etched into the foundation of our emotional selves, can shape our adult relationships in profound ways. As we explore the contours of attachment and vulnerability, the lens of psychology illuminates the paths we tread. But perhaps there's another layer to this narrative, one infused with divine insight.

Could it be that our spiritual compass guides us through the labyrinth, helping us find emotional grace and resilience, even in the face of past chaos? In this dance of psychology and spirituality, we find ourselves on a transformative journey, where ancient instincts, divine guidance, and the intricacies of modern dating converge, painting a vivid portrait of our pursuit of love and connection.

The Divine Psychological Journey

Final Bow and Curtain Call:

And there you have it, folks, our grand finale of the dating tango, orchestrated by none other than evolutionary psychology. As the curtains draw to a close, remember this: dating is a dance of evolution and choice, and you're the lead dancer. Embrace your quirks, navigate the changes, and laugh at the cosmic comedy. Because, let's face it, dating is like doing the cha-cha in roller skates – challenging, unpredictable, and at times, utterly hilarious.

So, as you venture out into the wild world of dating, go ahead, and do the Macarena of modern romance. Let your heart be your guide, let your mind be your navigator, and let evolution's tunes give your dance some extra groove. Who knows, you might just find your perfect dance partner, and together, you'll create a choreography that's uniquely yours. So, my friends, dance on, laugh on, and remember – love is the ultimate dance floor, and you're the star of the show!

The world will take you wherever you want to go.

Chapter 7-

MATERIALISM, PERCEPTION, AND SOCIAL ANXIETY

Alright, dear reader let's dive headfirst into the wild ride that is this book! Grab your metaphorical snorkel and buckle up for a journey through the uncharted waters of perception, psychology, and the unexpected twists of everyday life.

Picture this: you're in a supermarket, surrounded by a dazzling array of choices, feeling as if you're about to take on a grand quest rather than just grab a carton of milk. Crazy, right? But trust me, even mundane tasks have a way of revealing the fascinating dance between our minds, our emotions, and the world around us.

And speaking of dances, have you heard the one about the researcher who walked into a supermarket and tried to buy confidence along with the groceries? No? Well, you're in for a treat, because that's exactly what we're going to uncover in this chapter. But before we get all serious and dive into the complexities of social anxiety and perception, let's start with a laugh – because who says psychology can't have its own stand-up comedy show?

Did you hear about the cereal that started a band? It was great at making music, but terrible at making decisions – just like me in the cereal aisle!

Ok, maybe I'm not so good at delivering jokes.

Now, imagine standing in the cereal aisle, surrounded by a symphony of crunch and colour. As you scan the shelves, trying to decide on a box, you feel like you're auditioning for a reality show where the grand prize is the perfect breakfast. But hey, we've all been there, right? Who knew choosing cereal could be as nerve-wracking as deciding on a career path?

In this chapter, we're peeling back the layers of overwhelm, unpacking the science behind why the simplest tasks can feel like climbing Everest in stilettos. We'll uncover the psychological quirks that make us choose one cereal over another and how our brain's obsession with appearances might just be the star of the show.

And while we're at it, let's not forget the spotlight on social anxiety – that stage fright of the soul that turns even the most mundane interactions into nerve-racking performances. But fear not, we're diving into this sea of unease with floaties of knowledge and strategies for taming the butterflies in our stomachs.

So, get ready to contemplate, and maybe even have an "Aha!" moment or two. We're about to embark on a journey that's part stand-up comedy, part mind-bending exploration. And who knows, by the time we're done, you might just become the champion of the cereal aisle, the conqueror of social fears, and the master of your own perception. So, grab that shopping cart of curiosity, and let's roll down the aisle of insight together!

Take, for instance, a seemingly simple activity like going to the supermarket. Although you may not be directly interacting with people around you, they are still in close proximity. I have always felt a bit overwhelmed when I choose to go to a supermarket.

Overwhelm can be described as a feeling of being mentally or emotionally burdened to the point where one's ability to cope is significantly reduced. This might manifest as anxiety, stress, or even confusion.

In a supermarket, overwhelm might arise from various factors, such as sensory overload from bright lights and loud music, the sheer number of choices and decisions to be made, or the presence of many other shoppers.

For example, imagine standing in the cereal aisle, faced with countless options. As you scan the shelves, trying to decide which box to purchase, you feel the pressure mounting. The background noise of shopping carts, beeping registers, and other shoppers' conversations begin to merge into a cacophony that amplifies your discomfort. In that moment, even a simple decision feels paralyzing, and the weight of the situation bears down on you.

In today's consumer-driven world, the overwhelming variety of products and brands available at supermarkets can leave us feeling anxious and indecisive. Interestingly, our perception of the items we purchase is often intertwined with our own sense of identity and the way we believe others perceive us. For instance, some people choose more expensive brands over cheaper alternatives that serve the same purpose and contain similar ingredients. Why do we think this way? Is it because we believe that a higher price tag implies better quality, or is it due to concerns about our reputation and the judgments of others?

The Divine Psychological Journey

Illustration €

Supermarket dilemma

During my time in various supermarkets, I noticed that some high-end stores offer lower prices and better deals on select items. Intrigued by the psychology behind this phenomenon, I began to question whether our purchasing decisions are influenced by a subconscious concern for appearances. Do we, as consumers, care about what others think of the contents of our shopping carts?

I decided to conduct a social experiment to better understand this phenomenon. Over several months, I lowered my shopping standards and frequented lower-cost supermarkets. I dressed professionally and parked my rented luxury car as close to the entrance as possible, ensuring that both customers and staff members would notice me. Gradually, I began to interact with staff members and purchase non-branded items across a range of categories, from household goods to food and gardening tools.

As I transitioned from purchasing high-end items to more affordable, non-branded products, I felt a sense of shame, as though I were being judged by others however, I realized that, just like me, other shoppers were preoccupied with their own tasks and concerns. The overwhelming environment, with loud music, bustling crowds, and busy staff members, left little room for judgment. In fact, I discovered that my initial feelings of shame were rooted more in my own self-perception than in the opinions of others.

This experiment led me to confront my own preconceived notions about social judgments and appearances. While it is true that people may initially judge us based on our appearance or possessions, our behaviour can have a profound impact on their perceptions. A simple smile, a friendly conversation, or a kind gesture can quickly change someone's opinion of us. Our brains are wired to assess unknown people based on their appearance until we make a direct connection with them. Once that connection is made, our experience with the person can completely alter our perspective.

Social anxiety disorder, also known as social phobia, is a mental health condition characterized by an intense fear of being judged, negatively evaluated, or rejected in social situations. This fear can lead to feelings of embarrassment, self-consciousness, and avoidance of social activities. It is important to recognize that the fear of judgment is a natural and universal human experience, as it is rooted in our need to survive and thrive in society. However, when this fear becomes debilitating and prevents us from living a fulfilling life, it may be necessary to seek professional help to address and manage the condition.

The Divine Psychological Journey

This fear of judgment is deeply rooted in our need to survive and thrive in society, and it can lead to social anxiety disorder. This intense anxiety can interfere with daily activities, including work, school, and personal relationships. People with social anxiety disorder may avoid social situations altogether, or they may endure them with extreme discomfort.

Understanding and addressing the underlying factors contributing to social anxiety disorder can lead to healthier coping strategies and improved mental well-being. Cognitive-behavioural therapy (CBT) is one effective approach that helps individuals with social anxiety reframe their thoughts and perceptions of social situations, ultimately reducing their fear and anxiety.

In conclusion, my personal experiment in self-perception and social anxiety taught me that fearing judgment is a natural response related to our need to survive in society. However, it is essential to recognize that this fear often arises from our own negative self-image rather than the actual opinions of others. By embracing a positive attitude, engaging in genuine interactions, and focusing on our own behaviour, we can overcome the fear of judgment and embrace our authentic selves.

Culinary exploration

Chapter 8-

MAY I TAKE YOUR ORDER, PLEASE?

When we think of human behaviour, we often view it as a series of actions and decisions dictated by context, personal beliefs, and societal norms. Most of us follow patterns of behaviour that, over time, become routine. But what happens when someone consciously steps out of the realm of these typical routines? What happens when they choose to do something repetitive but unusual in the eyes of society?

Let's consider the "Culinary" experiment.

Illustration μ

The "Apple Pie" experiment

The experiment began as an exploration of this very question. Would a slight deviation from the norm, even if repetitive like other daily routines, elicit different responses from others? Moreover, would this different behaviour affect the person's perception of themselves or alter their interaction with the community?

In the experiment, I decided to visit a drive-through every day at 23:00 hours, ordering the same items: an apple pie and a small Fanta. Initially, it caused a slight disruption, as the apple pie wasn't readily available. But as the days passed, the staff adapted to my routine, even preparing the pie in anticipation of my order.

Then came the shift.

On the 13th day, as I pulled up to the window, I was met with laughter and playful taunts. The staff, recognizing me and my order, referred to me as "the apple pie guy" and made jokes about my unusual, albeit harmless, routine. This reaction reveals something crucial about societal norms and individual behaviour, as the laughter and playful jeers echoed from the drive-through window, a wave of unexpected emotions washed over me. I felt different, but not in a way I had anticipated.

There was an edge of discomfort, a prickling sense of being the odd one out. I felt singled out and, surprisingly, upset.

These feelings seemed odd to me. After all, I didn't personally know the restaurant's staff, and they didn't know me beyond my nightly order of an apple pie and a small Fanta. I hadn't done anything wrong, merely chosen a routine that was outside their expectations. But here I was, feeling as if I had been excluded from an unspoken community of 'normal' routine-keepers.

At that moment, I questioned why their response affected me so deeply. After some reflection, I came to understand a few crucial aspects of human psychology and social behaviour that might explain my emotional response.

Firstly, our perception of self is often influenced by how others perceive us. Known as 'reflected self-appraisal,' this concept suggests that we form our self-image based on how we think others see us. In this case, the staff's laughter and labelling of me as 'the apple pie guy' likely impacted my self-perception, leading to feelings of discomfort and difference.

Secondly, there's a fundamental human desire to belong, to be part of a group or community. This desire is so strong that exclusion or even the perception of being different can trigger feelings of distress or anxiety. This phenomenon, known as 'social pain,' is often equated to physical pain in terms of how our brain perceives it. It could explain why, despite not knowing the staff personally, their reaction made me feel upset.

However, this introspection allowed me to realize something essential - our emotional responses to such situations are entirely normal and natural. They're part of our social survival instincts, honed over millennia. But that doesn't mean we are bound by these reactions.

By understanding the psychological mechanisms at play, we can learn to manage these feelings. We can recognize that being different is not inherently bad, and that we can't please everyone. We can choose to live authentically, honouring our emotions and routines, irrespective of external judgements.

And, in doing so, we not only embrace our individuality but also foster a more inclusive community where everyone can be their unique selves. So, despite the initial discomfort, I continued to order my apple pie and Fanta, night after night, confident in my choice and hopeful of the acceptance I might inspire in others.

So, why do people react this way to deviations from the norm, even when those deviations are harmless?

From a psychological perspective, humans are social animals, wired to live and function within groups. This group living requires certain codes of conduct and unwritten rules, norms, which help maintain order and predictability. These norms differ from community to community, and they evolve over time.

When individuals conform to these norms, their behaviour is deemed predictable, and it comforts us. It suggests order, control, and social cohesion. However, when someone deviates from these norms, it disrupts this sense of predictability.

Even in the context of this experiment, where the deviation was harmless and routine in its own way, it was still outside the typical pattern expected by the restaurant staff. Their laughter and jesting can be seen as a form of social sanction - a light-hearted yet clear message indicating the recognition of this deviation.

But here's where the real insight lies.

In this enchanted experiment, the spotlight shines on the glorious art of emotional awareness and honesty. Picture this: to recognize our feelings amidst the tangled web of societal expectations is indeed a magical feat! It bestows upon us the power to boldly embrace our authentic selves, even in the face of raised eyebrows and snarky comments!

Behold the grand spectacle of this curious experiment, revealing an irony in our societal ways that'll tickle your fancy! Imagine this: we humans, delightful creatures of habit, go about our daily tasks on autopilot, hardly batting an eyelash. But hold on to your hats, the moment we dare to venture beyond the bounds of 'normal,' oh, how the eyes of scrutiny cast their judgment upon us!

But fret not, my curious readers, for the concept of 'normal' is but a sly chameleon, changing its hues with each twist and turn of culture. Being 'different,' my wonderful folks, is like a whimsical dance outside the lines of the current context. So, worry not, for what's 'normal' in this neck of the woods may be an entirely different tale in the far-off lands!

The Divine Psychological Journey

And so, my daring comrades, let us raise our banners of uniqueness high, for being 'different' is the spice that adds zest to the scrumptious buffet of life! Oh, yes, the laughter and judgment may come knocking, but fear not, for they are but the colourful strokes in the masterpiece of diversity that paints our society.

As long as our actions harm none and respect the rights of others, let us proudly wear the titles of the "apple pie guy," the "morning jogger," or the "night-time reader"! So fearlessly be you, embrace your quirks, and revel in the joy of being unapologetically YOU! For this whimsical journey is a merry ride, and together we shall laugh, love, and celebrate the splendid art of being 'different'! Onward, my extraordinary adventurers, for it's not just okay to be 'different,' it's a grand and marvellous adventure of a lifetime! Being 'different' is more than okay—it's an enchanting celebration of YOU!

Selfish chapter, my book my rules

Chapter 9-

DECISIONS IN THE HEART OF CARE: BALANCING LOGIC AND EMOTION

Ladies and gentlemen, gather 'round for a captivating exploration into the heart of decision-making. Picture this: a 26-year-old dementia care specialist, armed with empathy and logic, navigating the labyrinth of choices that define my professional journey. Join me as we unravel the intricate dance between emotional understanding and logical reasoning that shapes my path.

As a healthcare warrior, my arena is dementia care – a realm where every decision demands a blend of emotional intelligence and cool-headed logic. It's like being the conductor of a symphony, guiding my choices with a perfect harmony of compassion and intellect.

The Divine Psychological Journey

The Emotional Crescendo:

Empathy, patience, and kindness are my secret weapons, essential for deciphering the complex needs of my patients. It's a dance of understanding, where every sigh and every smile hold a story. Emotional decision-making transforms me from a nurse to a confidante, allowing me to heal not just the body, but also the soul.

However, life isn't a symphony with only one note. The symphony of decision-making also includes a logical sonata. I find myself standing at crossroads where factual data and reason are my guiding lights. It's like being the captain of a ship, steering through turbulent waters with a map of objective reasoning.

The Power of Leadership Choreography:

When I stand at the helm, a feeling of empowerment rushes through me. It's not about controlling others; it's about crafting a path that leads to positive outcomes. The thrill of making choices, solving puzzles, and catalysing change is my adrenaline rush. It's like being the protagonist in a choose-your-own-adventure story. THE MAIN CHARACTER SYNDROME?

This drive to lead and solve might have a psychological lineage called the 'need for achievement.' It's like a hidden compass that points me towards success. This compass comes from a deep-rooted urge to conquer tasks, crack problems, and scale the peaks of excellence.

The 'need for achievement' and the magical 'helper's high' twirl in the spotlight of my life decisions. The 'need for achievement' is my motivational anthem, pushing me to excel and redefine boundaries. It's like being an artist, constantly perfecting my masterpiece with each brushstroke of patient care.

Balancing on the Tightrope of Purpose:

But, ah, let's not forget that even the most exquisite dance requires balance. This relentless need for achievement can turn into an overzealous dance, leading to burnout. The applause of accomplishment can fade into exhaustion if not met with a standing ovation of self-care.

Ah, the 'helper's high,' where my heart finds its rhythm. Every patient I comfort, every soul I soothe, ignites a surge of euphoria. It's the brain's way of saying, "You did good, kid." It's like being sprinkled with fairy dust that lifts the spirit and adds a dash of sunshine to my day.

Yet, here's the twist: the applause should never drown out my own voice. The 'helper's high' shouldn't lead to neglecting the star of the show – me. Balancing the applause with self-care is like maintaining a seesaw. It's about understanding that helping others is my melody, but humming my own tune is equally vital.

The Divine Psychological Journey

Illustration *The Encore of Balance:*

Fig ≠

The Divine Psychological Journey

So, there you have it – my journey through the pages of balance, orchestrated by the 'need for achievement' and choreographed by the 'helper's high.' Like a conductor leading a symphony, I stand at the crossroads of emotion and reason. It's a dance of understanding and solving, a balance of caring and self-care.

Being in charge isn't just about leading—it's about understanding, empathising, solving, and caring. It's about making decisions that make a difference. And for me, that's what brings the most fulfilment.

And as the curtain falls, remember this: life's decisions are a dance were emotions waltz with logic. It's about being the conductor of your own symphony, striking the right balance between the heart's resonance and the mind's rhythm. So, my fellow decision-makers, dance on with empathy and logic, knowing that your symphony is uniquely yours to compose.

Disney I'm a big fan of you however…

Chapter 10-

LIGHTS, CAMERA, PSYCHOLOGICAL MANIPULATION

Ladies and gentlemen, boys and girls, gather 'round as we embark on an enchanting journey into the mesmerizing world of television. Let's think about Disney princesses, yeah, let's take it one by one. Picture this: a snowy kingdom where a fearless ice queen named Elsa casts a spell, a magical underwater realm where a curious mermaid named Ariel explores the unknown, and a quaint village where a book-loving belle named Belle seeks adventure. But is there more to these princesses than meets the eye? You bet your glass slipper there is! And that's what we're here to unravel – the psychological dimensions of these iconic characters and how they weave their way into our minds and hearts.

Which Disney Princes skills or traits have you got?

The Divine Psychological Journey

Illustration ă

Fig., 4x3=12

The Divine Psychological Journey

The Enchanted Princesses and Their Mind-Bending Traits:

Now, let's get down to business (to defeat the stereotypes). Our beloved Disney princesses aren't just pretty faces with sparkly gowns; they're complex characters who hold a mirror to the traits and struggles that make us human. As we journey through their tales, we discover the psychological roots that anchor us to their stories.

Cinderella – The Resilient Dreamer:

Cinderella, with her glass slipper and pumpkin carriage, teaches us that even when life throws us a wicked curveball, we can harness our resilience to transcend our circumstances. But what's the magic behind her enduring appeal? Psychologically, Cinderella taps into our innate longing for transformation and hope. Her rags-to-riches story resonates because it mirrors our own aspirations for a better life. Her resilience reminds us that even in the face of adversity, we can find the strength to pursue our dreams.

Ariel – The Curious Explorer:

Ariel's yearning to trade her fins for feet and explore the world above the waves speaks to our universal curiosity. Her adventurous spirit triggers our own desires for exploration and novelty. Psychologically, Ariel reflects the intrinsic human drive to expand our horizons, even if it means venturing into the unknown. Her journey resonates with our own quests for self-discovery, urging us to dive headfirst into uncharted waters.

Belle – The Intellectual Seeker:

Belle's love for books and her thirst for knowledge reflect our own human quest for understanding and connection. In her tale as old as time, she finds solace in stories and sees beyond appearances. Psychologically, Belle taps into our innate desire to connect deeply with others and break free from societal norms. Her evolution from bookworm to independent thinker resonates with our longing for authentic connections and personal growth.

Elsa – The Empowered Sovereign:

Now, let's fast forward to the icy realm ruled by Elsa, the Snow Queen. Her journey from self-imposed isolation to self-acceptance reverberates with our universal struggle for authenticity. Psychologically, Elsa's story aligns with our desire to break free from the constraints of societal expectations and embrace our true selves. Her anthem "Let It Go" serves as a reminder that letting go of fears and limitations can lead to personal liberation and empowerment.

Evolution in Disney Characters and Unveiling Stereotypes:

As we tiptoe through the tulips of Disney history, we uncover a fascinating evolution. The first Disney princesses, like Snow White and Sleeping Beauty, were often portrayed as damsels in distress, awaiting their prince to sweep them off their feet. But times have changed, my friends. Enter the new generation of Disney princesses like Elsa and Moana, who chart their destinies independently and redefine what it means to be a strong, empowered woman.

Let's not gloss over the psychological implications of these evolutions. The shift from passive dependence to active empowerment reflects society's own transformation. It challenges stereotypes that pigeonholed women into predefined roles and encourages us to rewrite our narratives. Just as Disney characters have grown, so have we – embracing our unique strengths and voices.

But wait, the magic doesn't end with character arcs and plot twists. Television, our modern-day genie, has its tricks up its remote-controlled sleeve. It uses a spellbinding combination of psychological tactics to sway our thoughts and emotions. Advertisements sprinkle glitter on products we never knew we needed, tapping into our desire for belonging and status. News programs grab our attention with sensationalism, fuelling our primal need for survival information.

Even our beloved Disney tales aren't immune. Psychologically, they capitalize on our yearning for connection, courage, and self-discovery. By weaving relatable emotions and universal themes into their stories, Disney hooks us – children and adults alike – and moulds our perceptions of love, strength, and identity.

As we conclude our exploration of the magic box and its enchantments, let's sprinkle a bit of pixie dust with some Disney humour. Why did Ariel decide to become a marine biologist? Because she wanted to learn about "fishology"! And how does Cinderella manage her time so effectively? She's the master of "pumpkin management"!

In jest, there's truth. Just as these quips tickle our funny bones, they remind us that life's complexities are meant to be navigated with a pinch of humour. As we venture forth, let's remember that while television may wield its psychological wand, we too hold our own wands of mindfulness and discernment.

Conclusion:

And so, dear reader, we bid adieu to this whirlwind tour of television's psychological dance. We've peeled back the layers of Disney princesses, explored the evolution of character stereotypes, and unmasked the secrets of television's mind manipulation. But fret not, for within these pages lies not just knowledge, but the power to see beyond the screen's illusion.

As we journey through this ever-changing landscape of pixels and narratives, let us be the masters of our own magic. Let's treasure the lessons and laughter, while keeping our eyes wide open to the art of persuasion. Remember, life's remote is in your hands – choose wisely and write your own story, for you are the ultimate narrator of your own fairy tale.

ERMM...?

Chapter 11-

INTUITION - SUFFOCATING OR DIVINE FEELINGS?

"Why did the psychic refuse to write a chapter about intuition and divine feelings? Because they had a terrible premonition that the punchline would be too 'spiritually' bad!"

Like my jokes. **Bad**

In the depths of our existence, where the mind and soul entwine, lie the enigmatic realms of intuition and inexplicable sensations. In this chapter, we shall embark on a journey through the intricate tapestry of human emotions, exploring the interplay between the psychological and the divine in our everyday experiences.

Connections and the Exchange of Energies with People:

Deep Conversations and Rapid Responses:

Have you ever engaged in a profound conversation where words flowed effortlessly, ideas interconnected seamlessly, and your responses seemed to emerge from the depths of your being without conscious thought? It's as if the connection with the other person ignited a mental symphony, where every note resonated in harmony. Such moments of profound connection often leave us pondering whether there's more to our interactions than meets the eye.

These instances of heightened connection are often attributed to the subconscious mind. Your brain is an intricate web of knowledge and experiences, and sometimes, in the presence of a kindred spirit, it can rapidly synthesize information and provide responses seemingly from thin air. This psychological phenomenon can feel almost mystical, but it is a testament to the incredible processing power of the human brain.

Emotions Unfiltered by Thought:

Goosebumps:

Imagine standing on a mountaintop, overlooking a breathtaking vista, and suddenly, your skin erupts in goosebumps. Or perhaps, you're listening to a spine-tingling piece of music, and the same phenomenon occurs. Goosebumps are often associated with a deep emotional response. But what causes this peculiar reaction, and could it be more than a simple physical response?

Goosebumps are a vestige of our evolutionary past. When we experience intense emotions, the tiny muscles at the base of our hair follicles contract, causing the hair to stand on end and creating goosebumps. This physiological response is a remnant of our ancestors' attempts to appear larger when threatened. While goosebumps are primarily a physical reaction, they can also be triggered by intense emotions, suggesting a deep connection between our physical and emotional states.

Emotions in a Spiritual Light:

Feelings of Oppression:

There are moments in life when a heavy, suffocating feeling settles upon us, seemingly out of nowhere. It's as though the weight of the world rests upon our shoulders. Is this purely a psychological response to stress, or could it be a signal from the universe, urging us to pay attention to something greater?

Feelings of oppression are often rooted in psychological stressors, such as anxiety or the burdens of daily life. They can manifest physically as a tightness in the chest or a sense of constriction. These sensations are typically a call to address underlying emotional or psychological issues rather than divine messages.

What was I on about?

Forgotten Knowledge:

How many times have you had the nagging feeling that you've forgotten something important, only for a significant event or revelation to occur shortly afterward? Is this a case of our subconscious mind alerting us to potential dangers, or could it be a whisper from the cosmos?

This sensation of forgetting something important can often be attributed to our subconscious mind processing information beyond our conscious awareness. It's as though our intuition is sending us a subtle signal, urging us to remain alert and attentive. While it might feel mystical, it's often the result of our brain's remarkable ability to connect the dots.

Anticipating the Future:

Feelings of Impending Good or Bad:

There are moments when an unshakable feeling settles in your gut, foretelling an impending event. It could be an ominous premonition of something bad or an overwhelming sense of impending good fortune. Is this a manifestation of your intuition or a psychological projection?

While science struggles to explain these intuitive sensations fully, many individuals attribute such premonitions to a heightened sense of intuition. Some believe that our inner selves can tap into a deeper well of knowledge, picking up on subtle cues and patterns in the universe. It's as though the cosmos sends us messages through our intuition, guiding us along our life's journey.

The Divine Psychological Journey

Illustration ✕

Connection between soul and brain

108

Shadows of the Unseen:

Perceiving the Inexistent:

Have you ever felt the presence of someone who isn't physically there? Perhaps a deceased loved one or an unseen companion? These experiences, while deeply personal, often lead to questions about whether they are the product of our psyche or glimpses into a spiritual realm.

These sensations, known as "presence hallucinations," are believed to arise from the brain's complex interplay of memory, emotion, and perception. In times of emotional distress or deep longing, our brain can create the illusion of the presence of a loved one as a source of comfort. While it might not be a divine visitation, it is a testament to the power of our emotions and memories.

The Divine Psychological Journey

As we navigate the profound intricacies of human psychology, we also uncover the boundless wonders of the human spirit. While science illuminates the rational explanations for many phenomena, it's important to remember that there exists a realm beyond, a world where intuition and the limitless potential of the human soul reign.

This divine psychological journey isn't merely an intellectual exploration; it's an invitation to commune with the deepest layers of our being. It's an odyssey that beckons us to embrace the magic and mystery that reside within us. This is where the ordinary transcends into the extraordinary, and where science and spirituality converge, weaving a tapestry of understanding that celebrates both the mind and the soul.

So, as we conclude this chapter, remember that the "The Divine Psychological Journey: Embracing Vulnerability" is your bridge between the known and the unknown, between the rational and the mystical. It's an affirmation that, in this intricate dance, we find the true essence of our humanity – a beautiful blend of the psychological and the divine.

> While science can provide rational explanations for many phenomena, there remains a profound mystery that invites us to explore the depths of our intuition and the limitless possibilities of the human soul.

FINALLY

Chapter 12-

A GRAND EXPERIMENT IN PERCEPTION

Ah, dear reader, we have arrived at the climax of our journey, where the threads of perception and understanding weave together in an intricate tapestry. As we prepare to bid adieu to these pages, let us embark on a final dance, a dance that challenges the very boundaries of our comprehension.

This book, my dear friend, has been more than a mere collection of chapters. It has been a grand experiment, a cerebral masquerade where words and ideas cavort like masked dancers, beguiling, and intriguing in equal measure. But, why, you may ask? Because, my fellow explorer, the heart of our journey lies not in the destination but in the journey itself.

Remember, at the outset, we delved into the enigma of perception, uncovering its powers and pitfalls. We learned how our minds paint the world around us, often using hues we aren't consciously aware of. And in this dance of perception, we realized that our own beliefs and biases often guide our choices and interactions.

Recall the tales of Disney princesses, those beloved characters who have waltzed through our collective imagination for generations. In their stories, we discovered reflections of different personality traits, strengths, and struggles. These princesses served as mirrors, echoing the complexities of the human experience. Yet, beneath their fairytale exteriors, we unearthed the psychological nuances that resonate with our own desires for independence, struggles with identity, and yearning for connection.

But wait, my astute companion, did you notice the subtle deviations from the norm? The deliberate diversions from conventional storytelling? The cunningly placed "easter eggs" that dared you to question your assumptions? This book, much like life itself, refused to adhere to the rigid choreography of expectations. The words on these pages tangoed to a rhythm of their own, inviting you to step outside the comfort of the known and embrace the thrill of uncertainty.

Now, a confession, my co-conspirator in this grand experiment: you, dear reader, have been an integral part of this dance. Your thoughts, emotions, and reactions have been the instruments in our symphony.

The Divine Psychological Journey

You journeyed through the corridors of perception, explored the landscapes of psychology, and questioned the very essence of narratives—both in fiction and reality.

Perhaps, in your exploration, you felt a tantalizing discomfort, a gentle pull at the edges of your understanding. This, my friend, is the curtain of normality we hang to shield ourselves from the capricious winds of the unknown. The deviations from the expected path, the disregard for convention, and the strategic placement of those "easter eggs" were all threads woven into this intricate fabric, beckoning you to embrace the intoxicating dance of the mind.

As we bid adieu to these pages, let us pause and savour the symphony of thoughts we've waltzed through. We pirouetted through the hallways of psychology, twirled through the tales of princesses, and danced along the labyrinth of perception. In this journey, we've unravelled the vivid tapestry of our humanity, resplendent with colours and textures that define who we are and who we aspire to be.

So, my fellow adventurer in this grand cerebral experiment, I leave you with a final embrace of words. May you continue to question, to dance, and to venture beyond the confines of the expected. As you navigate life's intricate dance, remember that the music of perception is ever evolving, the steps of connection are boundless, and the true beauty of understanding lies in daring to explore the unknown.

So, dance on, dear reader, dance on.

The Divine Psychological Journey

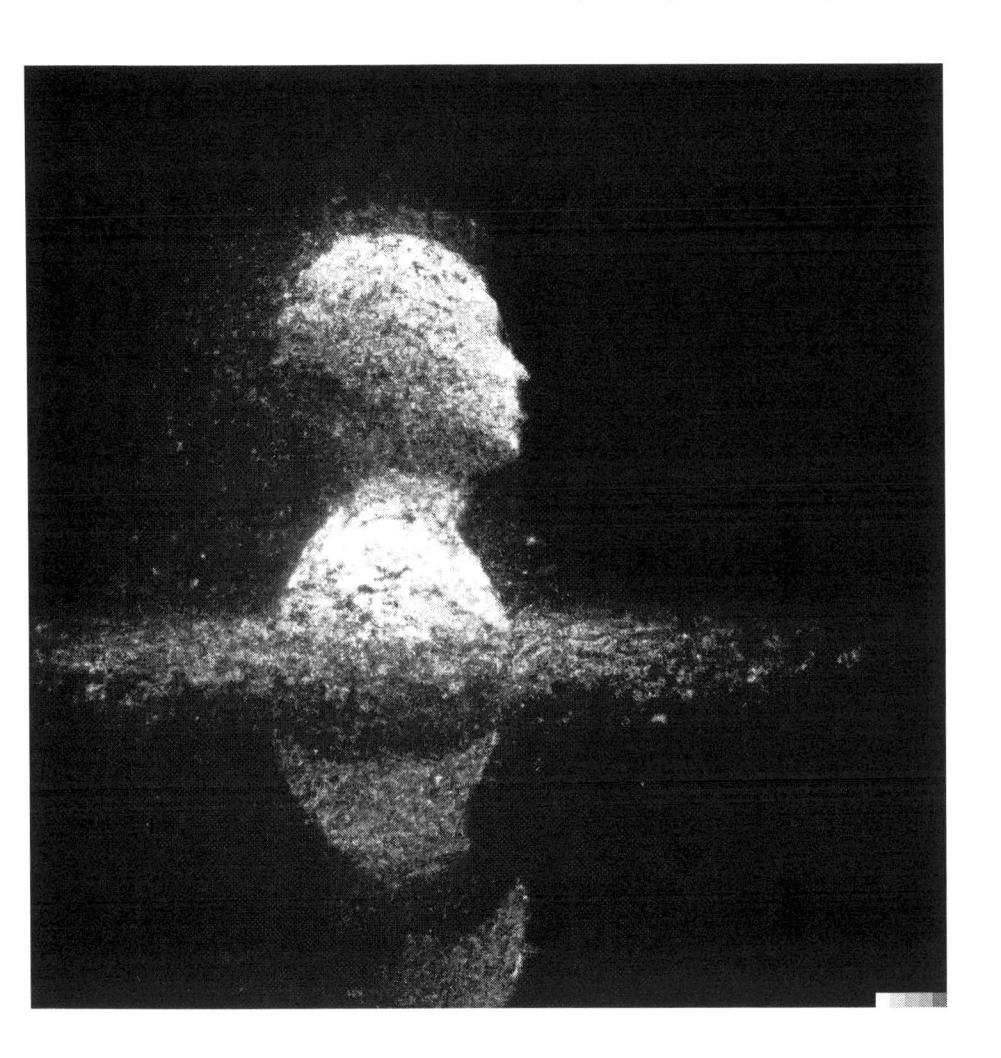

Illustration ∞

The Divine Psychological Journey

The end.

To You, Dear Reader,

As we reach the final page of this book, I want to extend my heartfelt gratitude to you. You, the intrepid explorer of words and ideas, have embarked on a remarkable journey with me through the labyrinth of perception, the psyche of Disney princesses, and the enigmatic threads of intuition and emotion.

Your participation in this grand experiment, your curiosity, and your willingness to delve into the depths of human nature have enriched this voyage in ways words can scarcely capture. It's readers like you who breathe life into the pages of a book, transforming it from mere text into a vibrant tapestry of shared experiences and insights.

I hope you've found moments of inspiration, reflection, and perhaps even a touch of amusement within these chapters. But most importantly, I hope you've discovered the magic of questioning, of dancing with uncertainty, and of embracing the infinite possibilities of perception and understanding.

Remember, dear reader, that you are a crucial part of this narrative, and your presence here has made it all the more profound. Your thirst for knowledge, your willingness to challenge the status quo, and your openness to explore the uncharted territories of the mind are the sparks that ignite change and growth.

As you close this book, know that your journey doesn't end here. It continues in the real world, where each interaction, each choice, and each moment become an opportunity to apply the insights you've gained. Embrace the beauty of understanding, continue to question, and always keep the music of perception playing in your heart.

Thank you for being a part of this extraordinary adventure. Your presence has made all the difference.

With deepest appreciation,

Ionuț-Alexandru Drăcea

The Divine Psychological Journey

The Divine Psychological Journey

In our next odyssey, we shall dive deeper.

"In the aftermath of our breakup, I struggled to come to terms with the idea that I might never find love again.

But as time passed, I realized that love is not a finite resource.

Loving one person doesn't mean that you can't love another.

While I haven't found another love, I've come to appreciate that the possibility of love still exists."

Stay tuned!

Printed in Great Britain
by Amazon